God Bless,

Betty Jo Woodham

PSALM 119

Oh How I Love Thy Word

Authored and Illustrated
By

Betty Jo Woodhouse

 Maximilian Press Publishers
920 S. Battlefield Blvd., suite 100
Chesapeake, Virginia 23322
757-482-2273

All Scripture is taken from the *Holy Bible*, Original King James Version.
Biblical names are taken from *Women in the Bible, Web Bible Encyclopedia.*

MAXIMILIAN PRESS PUBLISHERS and colophon
are registered trademarks of
Maximilian Press Publishing Company

Illustrations by Betty Jo Woodhouse, Copyright 2007
Edited by Betty Jo Woodhouse
Cover Design by Betty Jo Woodhouse

Manufactured in the United States of America

10 9 8 7 6 5 4 3 2 1

ISBN-13: 978-1-930211-81-0
ISBN-10: 1-930211-81-3

Paper used in this publication meets the minimum
requirements of ANSI/NISO Z39.48-1992 (1997)
(PERMANENCE OF PAPER)

Contents

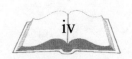

Dedication

*T*hank you God for the gift of Your Holy Word. Because of your limitless love, you sent Your Son Jesus Christ into the world and into my life. Your precious Holy Spirit and Your guidance encouraged me to illustrate Psalm 119 the way you saw befitting.

I dedicate this book to my mother Nona Bernice Collins, who was so incredibly gifted at interpreting God's Holy Word. Thank you "Mama" for encouraging me to be more like Jesus.

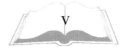

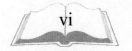

Acknowledgments

God will send special people into our lives to assist us in making our mental, creative, or artistic abilities come together. I want to extend my personal and sincere thanks to my family and friends.

DeCarlo Woodhouse– my youngest son, who has been blessed with many gifts. Your "spiritual wisdom" is beyond your years, and your writing skills are exceptional. Thanks for helping me bring it all together.

Calvin Woodhouse Jr.– my good-hearted and eldest son, without your patience, and "critical eye" this assignment would have taken me much longer to complete.

Calvin Woodhouse– for believing in me, and encouraging me to finish this project.

Rhonda Mealy–for helping me write my introduction, I needed your "English Teacher" know-how. Thanks!

Oh How I Love Thy Word

*O*ur "Master Creator" is most generous to give to the human race an inventive people called artists. And by that name we are blessed with the ability to design and create works of art that mankind can enjoy viewing for numerous years.

Betty Jo Woodhouse

And the Word was made flesh, and dwelt among us. (and we beheld His glory, the glory as of the only begotten of the Father,) full of grace and truth.

John 1:14

Introduction

"For unto us a child is born, unto us a son is given: and the government shall be upon his shoulder: and his name shall be called Wonderful, Counselor, The mighty God, The everlasting Father, The Prince of Peace." (Isaiah 9:6, KJV)

As prophesized, God's Word left heaven and came down to earth to give honor and purpose to God's Law. Jesus, acknowledged and received willingly the divine lineage and authority of the Law. Jesus stated, "Think not that I am come to destroy the law, or the prophets: I am not come to destroy, but to fulfill." (Mathew 5:17, KJV)

God's Word spoke to me when I was reading Psalm 119. Defined as a sacred song, or poetic composition, it was written to give God honor and praise. Psalms were written so that mankind would develop a commitment, a respect and submission to God's spoken Word. As the longest Psalm in the Bible, it also contains the most verses, thereby is credited as having the longest chapter. It's complexity lies in the twenty-two stanzas of alphabetic acrostics with one hundred and seventy-six verses that speak of God's power, His perfection, and the majesty of His Law. Words such as statues, commandments, testimony, and ordinances designate the "Law."

It is truly amazing how His Word moved me to demonstrate my love and admiration for Him and His Word. I dedicated myself to comprehend and transform God's Law into visual and spiritual personifications of His teachings. Because of His grace, I was inspired to create images of women who were representations of His divine Word. These women (i.e., Naomi, Judith, Eunice, etc.) each played a significant role in the Holy Bible in their own unique way. Therefore I have drawn in pen and ink twenty-two scenes of women who were enamored by His divine presence, a presence strong enough to engage the negative space and offer enlightenment to all who observe.

To spiritually bring forth this idea, I first began every new illustration with prayer giving honor and praise to God. Secondly, I asked the Holy Spirit for inspiration to create works that were pleasing to God. After all, He is my partner who instructs and walks beside me, and opens my mind to God's Word.

The illustrations of Psalm 119 are pages of praise and song for the one who has given us all life and life so abundantly. It is important that you view each illustration and read every line to this Psalm, so that you will be able to identify with every character using your life's experiences. May these words open your eyes to see the wondrous things He has done and will do for you. May the words and illustrations inspire you to trust and do something special for Our Master Creator.

Betty Jo Woodhouse

xiii

ABIGAIL
(Father's Joy)

1 Blessed are the undefiled in the way, who walk in the law of the Lord.

2 Blessed are they that keep his testimonies, and that seek him with the whole heart.

3 They also do no iniquity: they walk in his ways.

4 Thou hast commanded us to keep thy precepts diligently.

5 O that my ways were directed to keep thy statues!

6 Then shall I not be ashamed, when I have respect unto all thy commandments.

7 I will praise thee with uprightness of heart, when I shall have learned thy righteous judgments.

8 I will keep thy statues: O forsake me not utterly.

Blessed are the undefiled in the way, who walk in the law of the Lord.

JEHOSHEBA
(Oath to Jehovah)

9 Wherewithal shall a young woman cleanse her way? By taking heed thereto according to thy word.

10 With my whole heart have I sought thee: O let me not wander from thy commandments.

11 Thy word have I hid in mine heart, that I might not sin against thee.

12 Blessed art thou, O Lord: teach me thou statues.

13 With my lips have I declared all the judgments of thy mouth.

14 I have rejoiced in the way of thy testimonies, as much as in all riches.

15 I will meditate in thy precepts, and have respect unto thy ways.

16 I will delight myself in thy statues: I will not forget thy word.

With my whole heart have I sought thee; O let me not wander from thy commandments.

TIRZAH
(Delight)

17 Deal bountifully with thy servant, that I may live, and keep thy word.

18 Open thou mine eyes, that I may behold wondrous things out of thy law.

19 I am a stranger in the earth: hide not thy commandments from me.

20 My soul breaketh for the longing that it hath unto thy judgments at all times.

21 Thou hast rebuked the proud that are cursed, which do err from thy commandments.

22 Remove from me reproach and contempt; for I have kept thy testimonies.

23 Princes also did sit and speak against me: but thy servant did meditate in thy statues.

24 Thy testimonies also are my delight and my counselors.

Open thou mine eyes, that I may behold wondrous things out of thy law

SHIMRITH

(Vigilant)

25 My soul cleaveth unto the dust: quicken thou me according to thy word.

26 I have declared my ways, and thou heardest me: teach me thy statues.

27 Make me to understand the way of thy precepts: so shall I talk of thy wondrous works.

28 My soul melteth for heaviness: strengthen thou me according unto thy word.

29 Remove from me the way of lying: and grant me thy law graciously.

30 I have chosen the way of truth: thy judgments have I laid before me.

31 I have stuck unto thy testimonies: O Lord, put me not to shame.

32 I will run the way of thy commandments, when thou shalt enlarge my heart.

My soul melteth for heaviness: strengthen thou me according to thy word.

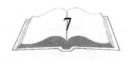

ISCAH

(One Who Looks Forth)

33 Teach me, O Lord, the way of thy statues; and I shall keep it unto the end.

34 Give me understanding, and I shall keep thy law; yea, I shall observe it with my whole heart.

35 Make me to go in the path of thy commandments; for therein do I delight.

36 Incline my heart unto thy testimonies, and not to covetousness.

37 Turn away mine eyes from beholding vanity; and quicken thou me in thy way

38 Stablish thy word unto thy servant, who is devoted to thy fear.

39 Turn away my reproach which I fear: for thy judgments are good.

40 Behold, I have longed after thy precepts: quicken me in thy righteousness.

Make me to go in the path of thy commandments; for therein do I delight.

JUDITH
(Praised)

41 Let thy mercies come also unto me, O Lord, even thy salvation, according to thy word.

42 So shall I have wherewith to answer him that reproacheth me: for I trust in thy word.

43 And take not thy word of truth utterly out of my mouth; for I have hoped in thy judgments.

44 So shall I keep thy law continually forever and ever.

45 And I will walk at liberty: for I seek thy precepts.

46 I will speak of thy testimonies also before kings, and will not be ashamed.

47 And I will delight myself in thy commandments, which I have loved.

48 My hands also will I lift up unto thy commandments, which I have loved; and I will meditate in thy statues.

My hands also will I lift up unto thy commandments, which I have loved; and I will meditate in thy statues.

SHOMER

(Keeper)

49 Remember the word unto thy servant, upon which thou hast caused me to hope.

50 This is my comfort in my affliction: for thy word hath quickened me.

51 The proud have had me greatly in derision: yet have I not declined from thy law.

52 I remembered thy judgments of old, O Lord; and have comforted myself.

53 Horror hath taken hold upon me because of the wicked that forsake thy law.

54 Thy statues have been my songs in the house of my pilgrimage.

55 I have remembered thy name, O Lord, in the night, and have kept thy law.

56 This I had, because I kept thy precepts.

I have remembered thy name, O Lord in the night, and have kept thy law.

THY WORD HATH QU
KEPT THY PRECE
O LORD REME
THY SERV
REMEMEM
THY NAM
MY COMFORTER M

SHIPHRAH

(Brightness)

57 Thou art my portion, O Lord: I have said that I would keep thy words.

58 I entreated thy favor with my whole heart: be merciful unto me according to thy word.

59 I thought on my ways, and turned my feet unto thy testimonies.

60 I made haste, and delayed not to keep thy commandments.

61 The bands of the wicked have robbed me: but I have not forgotten thou law.

62 At midnight I will rise to give thanks unto thee because of thy righteous judgments.

63 A am a companion of all them that fear thee, and of them that keep thy precepts.

64 The earth, O Lord, is full of thy mercy: teach me thy statues.

At midnight I will rise to give thanks unto thee because of thy righteous judgments.

SHELOMITH

(Peaceful)

65 Thou had dealt well with thy servant, O Lord, according unto thy word.

66 Teach me good judgment and knowledge: for I have believed thy commandments.

67 Before I was afflicted I went astray: but now have I kept thy word.

68 Thou art good, and doest good; teach me thy statues.

69 The proud have forged a lie against me: but I will keep thy precepts with my whole heart.

70 Their heart is as fat as grease; but I delight in thy law.

71 It is good for me that I have been afflicted; that I might learn thy statues.

72 The law of thy mouth is better unto me than thousands of gold and silver.

The proud have forged a lie against me: but I will keep thy precepts with my whole heart.

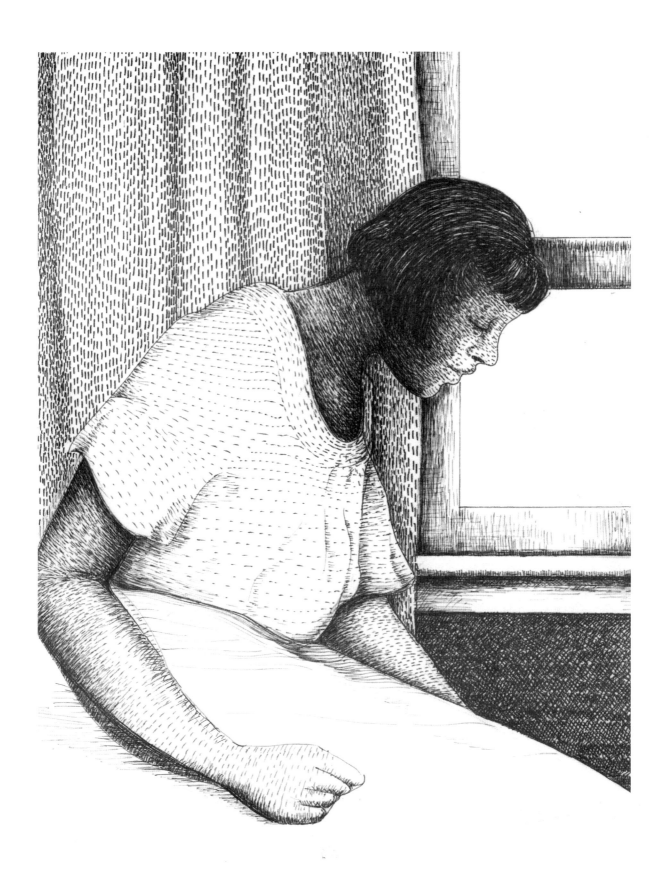

MARTHA

(A Lady)

73 Thy hands have made me and fashioned me: give me understanding, that I may learn thy commandments.

74 They that fear thee will be glad when they see me; because I have hoped in thy word.

75 I know, O Lord that thy judgments are right, and that thou in faithfulness hast afflicted me.

76 Let, I pray thee, thy merciful kindness be for my comfort, according to thy word unto thy servant.

77 Let thy tender mercies come unto me, that I may live: for thy law is my delight.

78 Let the proud be ashamed; for they dealt perversely with me without a cause: but I will meditate in thy precepts.

79 Let those that fear thee turn unto me, and those that have known thy testimonies.

80 Let my heart be sound in thy statues; that I be not ashamed.

Let the proud be ashamed; for they dealt perversely with me without a cause: but I will meditate in thy precepts.

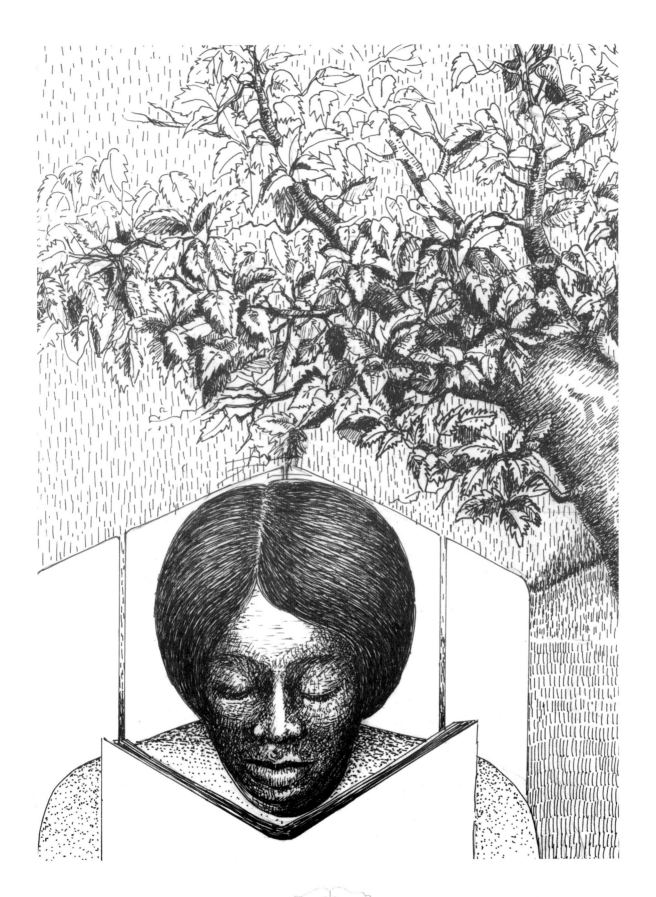

DINAH

(Judged and Acquitted)

81 My soul fainteth for thy salvation: but I hope in thy word.

82 Mine eyes fail for thy word, saying, when will thou comfort me?

83 For I am become like a bottle in the smoke; yet do I not forget that statues.

84 How many are the days of thy servant? When will thou execute judgment on them that persecute me?

85 The proud have digged pits for me, which are not after thy law.

86 All thy commandments are faithful: they persecute me wrongfully; help thou me.

87 They had almost consumed me upon earth; but I forsook not thy precepts.

88 Quicken me after thy loving kindness; so shall I keep the testimony of thy mouth.

All thy commandments are faithful: they persecute me wrongfully; help thou me.

MEHETABEL

(Favored by God)

89 Forever, O Lord, thy word is settled in heaven.

90 Thy faithfulness is unto all generations: thou hast established the earth, and it abideth.

91 They continue this day according to thine ordinances: for all are thy servants.

92 Unless thy law had been my delights, I should then have perished in mine affliction.

93 I will never forget thy precepts: for with them thou hast quickened me.

94 I am thine, save me; for I have sought thy precepts.

95 The wicked have waited for me to destroy me: but I will consider thou testimonies.

96 I have seen an end to all perfection: but thy commandment is exceeding broad.

I will never forget thy precepts: for with them thou hast quickened me.

ELISHEBA
(God is Her Oath)

97 O how I love thy law! It is my meditation all the day.

98 Thou through thy commandments hast made me wiser than mine enemies: for they are ever with me.

99 I have more understanding than all my teachers: for thy testimonies are my meditation.

100 I understand more than the ancients, because I keep thy precepts.

101 I have reframed my feet from every evil way, that I might keep thy word.

102 I have not departed from thy judgments: for thou hast taught me.

103 How sweet are thy words unto my taste! yea, sweeter than honey to my mouth!

104 Through thy precepts I get understanding: therefore I hate every false way.

I have more understanding than all my teachers: for thy testimonies are my meditations.

MESHULLEMETH

(Friend)

105 Thy word is a lamp unto my feet, and a light unto my path.

106 I have sworn, and I will perform it, that I will keep thy righteous judgments.

107 I am afflicted very much: quicken me, O Lord, according unto thy word.

108 Accept, I beseech thee, the freewill offerings of thy mouth, O Lord, and teach me thy judgments.

109 My soul is continually in my hand: yet do I not forget thy law.

110 The wicked have laid a snare for me: yet I erred not from thy precepts.

111 Thy testimonies have I taken as an heritage for ever: for they are the rejoicing of my heart.

112 I have inclined mine heart to perform thy statues alway, even unto the end.

Thy word is a lamp unto my feet, and a light unto my path.

27

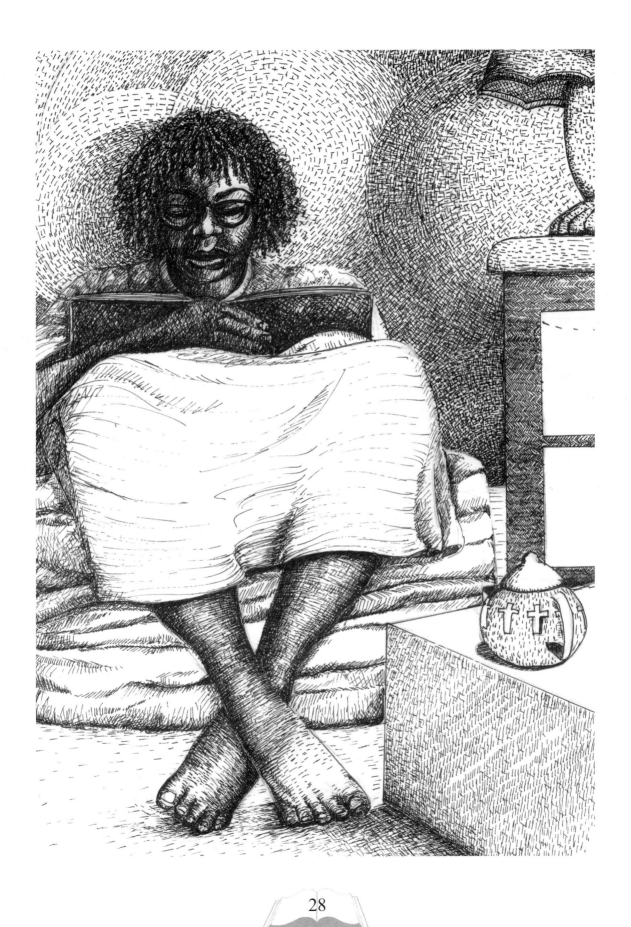

NAOMI

(My Pleasantness)

113 I hate vain thoughts: but thy law do I love.

114 Thou art my hiding place and my shield: I hope in thy word.

115 Depart from me, ye evildoers: for I will keep the commandments of my God.

116 Uphold me according unto thy word, that I may live: and let me not be ashamed of my hope.

117 Hold thou me up, and I shall be safe: and I will have respect unto thy statues continually.

118 Thou hast trodden down all them that err from thy statues: for their deceit is falsehood.

119 Thou puttest away all the wicked of the earth like dross: therefore I love thy testimonies.

120 My flesh trembleth for fear of thee; and I am afraid of thy judgments.

I hate vain thoughts: but thy law do I love.

HANNAH
(Graceful)

121 I have done judgment and justice: leave me not to mine oppressors.

122 Be surety for thy servant for good: let not the proud oppress me.

123 Mine eyes fail for thy salvation, and for the word of thy righteousness.

124 Deal with thy servant according unto thy mercy, and teach me thy statues.

125 I am thy servant; give me understanding, that I may know thy testimonies.

126 It is time for thee, Lord, to work: for they have made void thy law.

127 Therefore I love thy commandments above gold; yea, above fine gold.

128 Therefore I esteem all thy precepts concerning all things to be right; and I hate every false way.

I am thy servant; give me understanding, that I may know thy testimonies.

MARY

(A Tear)

129 Thy testimonies are wonderful: therefore doth my soul keep them.

130 The entrance of thy words giveth light; it giveth understanding unto the simple.

131 I opened my mouth, and panted: for I longed for thy commandments.

132 Look upon me, and be merciful unto me, as thou usest to do unto those that love thy name.

133 Order thy steps in thy word: and let not any iniquity have dominion over me.

134 Deliver me from the oppression of man: so will I keep thy precepts.

135 Make my face to shine upon thy servant; and teach me thy statues.

136 Rivers of water run down mine eyes, because they keep not thy law.

Rivers of waters run down mine eyes, because they keep not thy law.

PHEBE
(Pure and Bright)

137 Righteous art thou, O Lord, and upright are thy judgments.

138 Thy testimonies that thou hast commanded are righteous and very faithful.

139 My zeal hath consumed me, because my enemies have forgotten thy words.

140 Thy word is very pure: therefore thy servant loveth it.

141 I am small and despised: yet do not I forget thy precepts.

142 Thy righteousness is an everlasting righteousness, and thy law is the truth.

143 Trouble and anguish have taken hold on me: yet thy commandments are my delights.

144 The righteousness of thy testimonies is everlasting: give me understanding, and I shall live.

I am small and despised: yet do not I forget thy precepts.

35

DEBORAH

(Industrious)

145 I cried with my whole heart; hear me, O Lord: I will keep thy statues.

146 I cried unto thee; save me, and I shall keep thy testimonies.

147 I prevented the dawning of the morning, and cried: I hoped in thy word.

148 Mine eyes prevent the night watches, that I might meditate in thy word.

149 Hear my voice according to thy lovingkindness: O Lord, quicken me according to thy judgment.

150 They draw nigh that follow after mischief: they are far from thy law.

151 Thou art near, O Lord; and all thy commandments are truth.

152 Concerning thy testimonies, I have known of old that thou hast founded them forever.

I prevented the dawning of the morning, and cried: I hoped in thy word.

MAACHAH
(Oppression)

153 Consider mine affliction, and deliver me: for I do not forget thy law.

154 Plead my cause, and deliver me: quicken me according to thy word.

155 Salvation is far from the wicked: for they seek not thy statues.

156 Great are thy tender mercies, O Lord: quicken me according to thy judgments.

157 Many are my persecutors and mine enemies; yet do I not decline from thy testimonies.

158 I beheld the transgressors, and was grieved; because they kept not thy word.

159 Consider how I love thy precepts: quicken me, O Lord, according to thy lovingkindness.

160 Thy word is true from the beginning: and every one of thy righteous judgments endureth forever.

Many are my persecutors and mine enemies; yet do I not decline from thy testimonies.

MICHAIAH

(Who is Like God)

161 Princes have persecuted me without a cause: but my heart standeth in awe of thy word.

162 I rejoice at thy word, as one that findeth great spoil.

163 I hate and abhor lying: but thy law do I love.

164 Seven times a day do I praise thee because of thy righteous judgments.

165 Great peace have they which love thy law: and nothing shall offend them.

166 Lord, I have hoped for thy salvation, and done thy commandments.

167 My soul hath kept thy testimonies; and I love them exceedingly.

168 I have kept thy precepts and thy testimonies: for all my ways are before thee.

Great peace have they which love thy law: and nothing shall offend them.

EUNICE

(Good Victory)

169 Let my cry come near before thee, O Lord: give me understanding according to thy word.

170 Let my supplication come before thee: deliver me according to thy word.

171 My lips shall utter praise, when thou hast taught me thy statues.

172 My tongue shall speak of thy word: for all thy commandments are righteousness.

173 Let thine hand help me; for I have chosen thy precepts.

174 I have longed for thy salvation, O Lord; and thy law is my delight.

175 Let my soul live, and it shall praise thee; and let thy judgments help me.

176 I have gone astray like a lost sheep; seek thy servant; for I do not forget thy commandments.

My lips shall utter praise, when thou hast taught me thy statues.

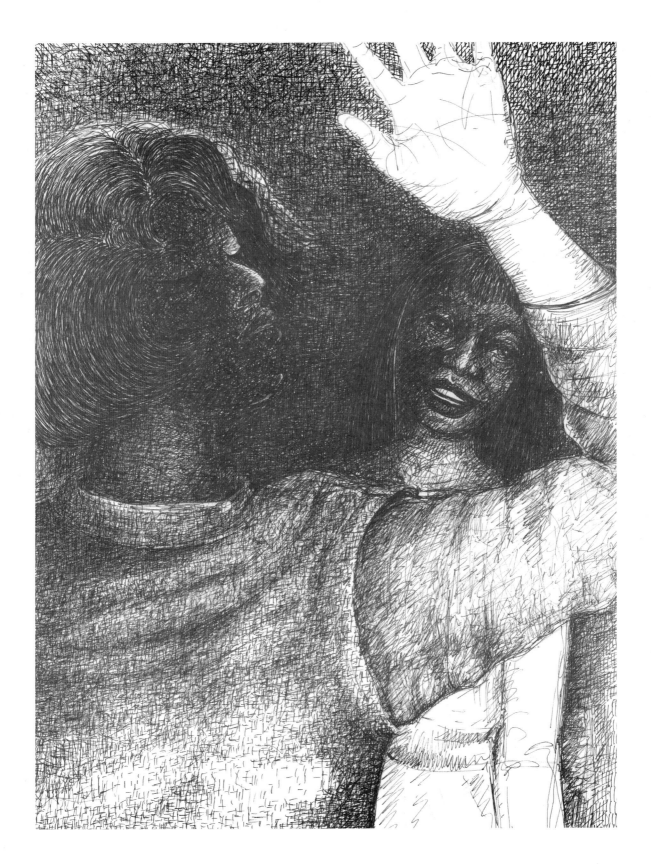